Vegan Stir Fry
2nd edition

By Don Orwell

http://SuperfoodsToday.com

Copyright © 2018 by Don Orwell.

All legal rights reserved. You cannot offer this book for free or sell it. You do not have reselling legal rights to this book. This eBook may not be recreated in any file format or physical format without having the expressed written approval of Don Orwell. All Violators will be sued.

While efforts have been made to assess that the information contained in this book is valid, neither the author nor the publisher assumes any accountability for errors, interpretations, omissions or usage of the subject matters herein.

Disclaimer:

The Information presented in this book is created to provide useful information on the subject areas discussed. The publisher and author are not accountable for any particular health or allergic reaction needs that may involve medical supervision and are not liable for any damage or damaging outcomes from any treatment, application or preparation, action, to any person reading or adhering to the information in this book. References are presented for informational reasons only and do not represent an endorsement of any web sites or other sources. Audience should be informed that the websites mentioned in this book may change.

This publication includes opinions and ideas of its author and is meant for informational purposes only. The author and publisher shall in no event be held liable for any damage or loss sustained from the usage of this publication.

Your Free Gift

As a way of saying thanks for your purchase, I'm offering you my FREE eBook that is exclusive to my book and blog readers.

Superfoods Cookbook - Book Two has over 70 Superfoods recipes and complements Superfoods Cookbook Book One and it contains Superfoods Salads, Superfoods Smoothies and Superfoods Deserts with ultra-healthy non-refined ingredients. All ingredients are 100% Superfoods.

It also contains Superfoods Reference book which is organized by Superfoods (more than 60 of them, with the list of their benefits), Superfoods spices, all vitamins, minerals and antioxidants. Superfoods Reference Book lists Superfoods that can help with 12 diseases and 9 types of cancer.

http://www.SuperfoodsToday.com/FREE

Table of Contents

Vegan Stir Fry.. 1

Introduction.. 5

Vegan Stir Fry Recipes 6

    Superfoods Stir Fry Marinade... 6

    Korean Spicy Stir Fry Marinade 7

    Garbanzo Stir Fry 8

    Vegan Stir Fry... 10

    Eggplant, Chinese Celery & Peppers Stir Fry 11

    Green Superfoods Stir Fry 12

    Cauliflower & Shiitake Stir Fry.. 13

    Onions, Lentils & Tomatoes Stir Fry 14

    Eggplant, Mushrooms & Carrots Stir Fry.............................. 15

    Baby Corn, Mushrooms & Asparagus Stir Fry 16

    Bamboo Shoots & Chinese Celery Stir Fry........................... 17

    Okra, Sprouts & Onions Choy Stir Fry 18

    Bok Choy & Seaweed Stir Fry 19

    Mushrooms, Snow Peas & Bok Choy Stir Fry 20

    Eggplant, Red Peppers & Carrots Stir Fry 21

    Eggplant, Shiitake & Bamboo Shoots Stir Fry..................... 22

    Zucchini, Peppers, Carrots, Mushrooms & Green Beans Stir Fry 23

    Bok Choy, Celery & Onions Stir Fry..................................... 24

    Mushrooms, Snow Peas & Broccoli Stir Fry 25

    Yellow Squash, Zucchini, Eggplant & Onions Stir Fry 26

Shiitake, GreenPeppers & Bamboo Shoots Stir Fry 27

Asparagus, Yellow Peppers & Tomato Stir Fry 28

Bok Choy, Almonds, Onions & Sesame Stir Fry 29

Broccolini, Zucchini, Tomatoes & Onions Stir Fry 30

Eggplant, Mushrooms, Carrots & Snow Peas Stir Fry 31

Red Peppers, Yellow Peppers & Olives Stir Fry 32

Broccoli, Green Onions & Red Peppers Stir Fry 33

Fennel, Bok Choy, Red Pepper & Celery Stir Fry 34

Kale & Pumpkin Stir Fry 35

Cauliflower & Green Onions Stir Fry 36

Kale & 2 Mushrooms Stir Fry 37

Kale, Carrot & Green Peas Stir Fry 38

Water Chestnut, Broccoli, Carrots, Snow Peas & Shrimp Stir Fry 39

Yellow Squash, Broccoli, Snow Peas & Shiitake Stir Fry 40

Zucchini, Green Beans, Leeks & Shrimp Stir Fry 41

Green Beans, Sesame, Broccoli, Red Peppers & Portobello Stir Fry .. 42

Shiitake, Bamboo Shoots & Eggplant Stir Fry 43

Superfoods Reference Book 44

Other Books from this Author 46

Introduction

Hello,

My name is Don Orwell and I had some life changing experiences in 2009 and that led me to start rethinking my eating habits and my current lifestyle. I have written a bunch of Superfoods related books (Superfoods Diet, Smart Carbs Detox, Superfoods Cookbook, a few books with Smoothies recipes, Superfoods Salads, Nighttime Eater, Superfoods Body Care etc.) and finally I have decided to expand my stir fry recipes collection and publish a Vegan Superfoods Stir Fry book. All ingredients in all recipes are 100% Superfoods. Enjoy!!

Vegan Stir Fry Recipes

Allergy labels: SF – Soy Free, GF – Gluten Free, DF – Dairy Free, EF – Egg Free, V - Vegan, NF – Nut Free

Superfoods Stir Fry Marinade

This marinade has 100% Superfoods ingredients and it's great with any meat or fish and even veggies. Sesame oil and sesame seeds are Superfoods, just like ginger, garlic, scallions, black pepper and red hot chili flakes. I personally don't use soy at all and I replaced soy sauce with fish sauce but you can use soy sauce if you want. Red wine is also Superfood rich in anthocyanidins, quercetin and resveratrol.

- 3 tbsp. soy sauce
- 2 tsp. sesame oil
- 1 tsp. freshly grated ginger
- 1 garlic clove, diced
- 1/4 cup red wine or vegetable broth or both

Optional:
- 1 Tbsp. arrowroot flour - if you want your stir fry thicker
- 1/4 cup chopped scallions
- 1 tsp. chili flakes (adjust for heat)
- 1/2 tsp. ground black pepper

Korean Spicy Stir Fry Marinade

- 3 tbsp. soy sauce
- 1 tsp. sesame oil
- 1 tsp. freshly grated ginger
- 1 garlic clove, diced
- 1 tsp. chili flakes or powder (adjust for heat)

Garbanzo Stir Fry

Serves 2

Ingredients - Allergies: SF, GF, DF, EF, V, NF

- 2 tbsp. oil
- 1 tbsp. oregano
- 1 tbsp. chopped basil
- 1 clove garlic, crushed
- ground black pepper to taste
- 2 cups cooked garbanzo beans

- 1 large zucchini, halved and sliced
- 1/2 cup sliced mushrooms
- 1 tbsp. chopped cilantro
- 1 tomato, chopped

Heat oil in a skillet over medium heat. Stir in oregano, basil, garlic and pepper. Add the garbanzo beans and zucchini, stirring well to coat with oil and herbs. Cook for 10 minutes, stirring occasionally. Stir in mushrooms and cilantro; cook 10 minutes, stirring occasionally. Place the chopped tomato on top of the mixture to steam. Cover and cook 5 minutes more.

VEGAN STIR FRY

Vegan Stir Fry
Serves 2

Ingredients - Allergies: SF, GF, DF, EF, V

- 1/2 pound shiitake mushrooms
- 1/2 cup Chinese Celery
- 1/2 cup sliced carrots and cucumbers
- 1 Tsp. oil

Instructions

Marinade mushrooms in a Superfoods marinade. Stir fry drained mushrooms in coconut oil for few minutes, add all other vegetables and stir fry for 2 more minutes. Add the rest of the marinade and stir fry for a minute. Serve with brown rice or quinoa.

Eggplant, Chinese Celery & Peppers Stir Fry
Serves 2

Ingredients - Allergies: SF, GF, DF, EF, V

- 1/2 pound cubed eggplant
- 1/2 cup Chinese Celery
- 1/2 cup sliced Red Peppers
- 1/4 cup sliced chili Peppers
- 1 Tsp. oil

Instructions

Marinade eggplant in a Superfoods marinade. Stir fry drained eggplant in coconut oil for few minutes, add all vegetables and stir fry for 2 more minutes. Add the rest of the marinade and stir fry for a minute. Serve with brown rice or quinoa.

Green Superfoods Stir Fry
Serves 2

Ingredients - Allergies: SF, GF, DF, EF

- 1/2 cup Kale
- 1/2 cup Chinese Celery
- 1/2 cup shiitake Mushrooms
- 1/2 cup sliced Bok Choy
- 1/2 cup Asparagus
- 1 Tsp. oil

Instructions

Marinade Asparagus and Kale in a Superfoods marinade. Stir fry drained Asparagus in coconut oil for few minutes, add all other vegetables and stir fry for 2 more minutes. Add the rest of the marinade and stir fry for a minute. Serve with brown rice or quinoa.

Cauliflower & Shiitake Stir Fry
Serves 2

Ingredients - Allergies: SF, GF, DF, EF

- 2 cups Cauliflower
- 1 cup sliced Shiitake mushrooms
- 1/2 cup sliced Green beans
- 1/2 cup sliced Broccoli
- 1/2 cup sliced carrot
- 1 Tbsp. coconut oil

Instructions

Stir fry cauliflower and broccoli in coconut oil for few minutes, add carrots and green beans and stir fry for 2 more minutes. Add the mushrooms and stir fry for 3 minutes more. Serve with brown rice or quinoa.

Onions, Lentils & Tomatoes Stir Fry

Serves 2

Ingredients - Allergies: SF, GF, DF, EF

- 1/2 pound cooked lentis
- 1 cup sliced Onions
- 1/2 cup sliced parsley
- 1/2 cup sliced carrots and Celery
- 1 Tsp. oil

Instructions

Add all vegetables and stir fry for 2 more minutes. Add the lentils and stir fry for a minute. Serve with brown rice or quinoa.

Eggplant, Mushrooms & Carrots Stir Fry
Serves 2

Ingredients - Allergies: SF, GF, DF, EF

- 1/2 pound sliced Eggplant
- 1 cup sliced Mushrooms
- 1/4 cup Basil leaves
- 1/2 cup sliced carrots and red peppers
- 1 Tsp. oil

Instructions

Marinade eggplant in a Superfoods marinade. Stir fry drained eggplant in coconut oil for few minutes, add all vegetables and stir fry for 2 more minutes. Add the rest of the marinade and stir fry for a minute. Serve with brown rice or quinoa.

Baby Corn, Mushrooms & Asparagus Stir Fry
Serves 2

Ingredients - Allergies: SF, GF, DF, EF

- 1 cup mushrooms
- 1/2 cup Baby corn
- 1/2 cup sliced green beans
- 1/2 cup sliced yellow peppers
- 1/2 cup asparagus
- 1 Tsp. oil

Instructions

Stir fry asparagus, green beans and baby corn in coconut oil for few minutes, add peppers and mushrooms and stir fry for 2 more minutes. Add the superfoods marinade and stir fry for a minute. Serve with brown rice or quinoa.

Bamboo Shoots & Chinese Celery Stir Fry
Serves 2

Ingredients - Allergies: SF, GF, DF, EF

- 3 cups sliced bamboo shoots
- 2 cups sliced Chinese celery
- 1/2 cup sliced onions
- 1 Tbsp. coconut oil

Instructions
Stir fry bamboo shoots in coconut oil for few minutes, add Chinese celery and onions and stir fry for 2 more minutes. Add the superfoods marinade and stir fry for a minute. Serve with brown rice or quinoa.

Okra, Sprouts & Onions Choy Stir Fry
Serves 2

Ingredients - Allergies: SF, GF, DF, EF

- 1 + 1/2 pound sliced okra
- 1 cup sprouts
- 1/2 cup sliced onions
- 1 Tbsp. coconut oil

Instructions

Marinade okra in a Superfoods marinade. Stir fry drained okra in coconut oil for few minutes, add onions and stir fry for 2 more minutes. Add the rest of the marinade and sprouts and stir fry for a minute. Serve with brown rice or quinoa.

Bok Choy & Seaweed Stir Fry
Serves 2

Ingredients - Allergies: SF, GF, DF, EF

- 2 cups sliced Bok Choy
- 1/2 cup dried mixed seaweed
- 1/2 cup julienned carrots
- 2 tbsp. bonito flakes
- 1 Tbsp. coconut oil

Instructions
Put the dried seaweed in lots of water and soak for 10-15 minutes. At the same time marinade sliced bok choy in Superfoods marinade for 15 minutes. Stir fry drained bok choy in coconut oil for 1 minute, add carrots, squeezed out seaweed and the rest of the marinade and stir fry for 1 more minute. Top with bonito flakes. Serve with brown rice or quinoa.

Mushrooms, Snow Peas & Bok Choy Stir Fry
Serves 2

Ingredients - Allergies: SF, GF, DF, EF

- 1/2 pound mushrooms
- 1 cup Snow Peas
- 1 cup sliced Bok Choy
- 1/2 cup sliced onions
- 1 Tbsp. coconut oil

Instructions

Marinade mushrooms in a Superfoods marinade. Stir fry drained mushrooms in coconut oil for few minutes, add onions and Snow Peas and stir fry for 2 more minutes. Add the rest of the marinade and bok choy and stir fry for a minute. Serve with brown rice or quinoa.

Eggplant, Red Peppers & Carrots Stir Fry
Serves 2

Ingredients - Allergies: SF, GF, DF, EF
- 1/2 pound Red Peppers
- 1 + 1/2 cup sliced Eggplant
- 1 cup sliced Carrots
- 1/2 cup sliced onions
- 1 Tbsp. coconut oil

Instructions
Marinade eggplant in a Superfoods marinade. Stir fry drained eggplant and carrots in coconut oil for 5 minutes, add red peppers and onions, stir fry for 2 more minutes. Add the rest of the marinade and stir fry for a minute. Serve with brown rice or quinoa.

Eggplant, Shiitake & Bamboo Shoots Stir Fry
Serves 2

Ingredients - Allergies: SF, GF, DF, EF

- 1/2 pound sliced shiitake mushrooms
- 1 cup sliced eggplant
- 1 cup sliced Green peppers
- 1/2 cup sliced carrots
- 1/2 cup sliced onions
- 1/2 cup sliced bamboo shoots
- 1 Tbsp. coconut oil

Instructions

Marinade shiitake, bamboo shoots and eggplant in a Superfoods marinade. Stir fry drained eggplant and bamboo shoots in coconut oil for 5 minutes, add carrots and onions and stir fry for 2 more minutes. Add the rest of the marinade with shiitake and stir fry for a minute. Serve with brown rice or quinoa.

Zucchini, Peppers, Carrots, Mushrooms & Green Beans Stir Fry

Serves 2

Ingredients - Allergies: SF, GF, DF, EF

- 1/2 cup sliced mushrooms
- 1/2 cup sliced Red Peppers
- 1/2 cup sliced Zucchini
- 1/2 cup sliced carrots
- 1/2 cup sliced green beans
- 1/2 cup sliced green onions
- 1 Tbsp. coconut oil

Instructions

Marinade zucchini in a Superfoods marinade. Stir fry drained zucchini in coconut oil for few minutes, add all other veggies and stir fry for 4 more minutes. Add the rest of the marinade and stir fry for a minute. Serve with brown rice or quinoa.

Bok Choy, Celery & Onions Stir Fry
Serves 2

Ingredients - Allergies: SF, GF, DF, EF

- 1/2 pound Bok Choy, sliced
- 1 cup sliced Celery
- 1/2 cup chopped onions
- 1 Tbsp. coconut oil

Instructions

Marinade white part of bok choy in a Superfoods marinade. Stir fry drained bok choy in coconut oil for 2 minutes, add celery and onions and stir fry for 2 more minutes. Add sliced green parts of bok choy and the rest of the marinade and stir fry for a minute. Serve with brown rice or quinoa.

Mushrooms, Snow Peas & Broccoli Stir Fry
Serves 2

Ingredients - Allergies: SF, GF, DF, EF

- 1/2 pound mushrooms
- 1 cup sliced Broccoli
- 1/2 cup sliced snow peas
- 1 Tbsp. coconut oil

Instructions

Marinade mushrooms in a Superfoods marinade. Stir fry drained mushrooms in coconut oil for few minutes, add broccoli and snow peas and stir fry for 2 more minutes. Add the rest of the marinade and stir fry for a minute. Serve with brown rice or quinoa.

Yellow Squash, Zucchini, Eggplant & Onions Stir Fry

Serves 2

Ingredients - Allergies: SF, GF, DF, EF

- 1/4 pound zucchini
- 1/4 pound yellow squash
- 1 cup sliced eggplant
- 1/2 cup sliced onions
- 1 Tbsp. coconut oil

Instructions

Marinade eggplant, squash and zucchini in a Superfoods marinade. Stir fry drained veggies in coconut oil for few minutes, add onions and stir fry for 2 more minutes. Add the rest of the marinade and stir fry for a minute. Serve with brown rice or quinoa.

Shiitake, GreenPeppers & Bamboo Shoots Stir Fry
Serves 2

Ingredients - Allergies: SF, GF, DF, EF
- 1/2 pound shiitake
- 1/2 cup sliced black mushrooms
- 1/2 cup sliced green peppers
- 1/2 cup sliced dried bamboo shoots
- 1 Tbsp. coconut oil

Instructions
Marinade shiitake in a Superfoods marinade. Stir fry drained shiitake in coconut oil for few minutes, add broccoli and water chestnuts and stir fry for 2 more minutes. Add the rest of the marinade and stir fry for a minute. Serve with brown rice or quinoa.

Asparagus, Yellow Peppers & Tomato Stir Fry
Serves 2

Ingredients - Allergies: SF, GF, DF, EF

- 1/2 pound asparagus
- 1 cup sliced Yellow peppers
- 1 cup chopped tomato
- 1 Tbsp. coconut oil

Instructions

Marinade asparagus in a Superfoods marinade. Stir fry drained asparagus in coconut oil for 7-8 minutes, add peppers and tomato and stir fry for 2 more minutes. Add the rest of the marinade and stir fry for a minute. Serve with brown rice or quinoa.

Bok Choy, Almonds, Onions & Sesame Stir Fry
Serves 2

Ingredients - Allergies: SF, GF, DF, EF

- 1/2 pound bok choy
- 1 + ½ cup sliced onions
- 3 Tbsp. almond slices
- 1 Tbsp. sesame seeds
- 1 Tbsp. coconut oil

Instructions

Marinade bok choy in a Superfoods marinade. Stir fry drained bok choy and onions in coconut oil for few minutes, add almond and sesame seeds and stir fry for 2 more minutes. Add the rest of the marinade and stir fry for a minute. Serve with brown rice or quinoa.

Broccolini, Zucchini, Tomatoes & Onions Stir Fry

Serves 2

Ingredients - Allergies: SF, GF, DF, EF

- 1/2 pound broccolini
- 1 cup sliced zucchini
- 3/4 cup sliced onions
- 3/4 cup chopped tomato
- 1 Tbsp. coconut oil

Instructions

Marinade broccolini in a Superfoods marinade. Stir fry drained broccolini in coconut oil for few minutes, add zucchini and onions and stir fry for 2 more minutes. Add tomatoes and the rest of the marinade and stir fry for a minute. Serve with brown rice or quinoa.

Eggplant, Mushrooms, Carrots & Snow Peas Stir Fry
Serves 2

Ingredients - Allergies: SF, GF, DF, EF

- 1/2 pound eggplant
- 1 + 1/2 cup mushrooms
- 1/2 cup sliced carrot
- 1 cup sliced snow peas
- 1 minced garlic clove
- 1 Tbsp. coconut oil

Instructions

Marinade eggplant in a Superfoods marinade. Stir fry drained eggplant in coconut oil for few minutes, add carrot, snow peas and garlic and stir fry for 2 more minutes. Add the rest of the marinade and stir fry for a minute. Serve with brown rice or quinoa.

Red Peppers, Yellow Peppers & Olives Stir Fry
Serves 2

Ingredients - Allergies: SF, GF, DF, EF

- 1 cup red peppers
- 1 cup green peppers
- 1 cup yellow peppers
- 1/2 cup carrot
- 1 rosemary sprig
- 1 Tbsp. basil leaves
- 1/2 cup olives
- 1 Tbsp. coconut oil

Instructions
Marinade all 3 types of peppers in a Superfoods marinade. Stir fry drained peppers and carrot in coconut oil for few minutes, add olives and rosemary and stir fry for 4-5 more minutes. Add the rest of the marinade and basil stir fry for a minute. Serve with brown rice or quinoa.

Broccoli, Green Onions & Red Peppers Stir Fry
Serves 2

Ingredients - Allergies: SF, GF, DF, EF

- 1/2 pound broccoli, with stalks peeled
- 1 cup red peppers
- 1 cup green onions
- 1 Tbsp. coconut oil

Instructions
Marinade peeled and sliced broccoli stalks in a Superfoods marinade. Stir fry drained broccoli stalks, broccoli florets and red peppers in coconut oil for 4-5 more minutes. Add the rest of the marinade, green onions and stir fry for a minute. Serve with brown rice or quinoa.

Fennel, Bok Choy, Red Pepper & Celery Stir Fry
Serves 2

Ingredients - Allergies: SF, GF, DF, EF

- 1 cup sliced celery
- 1 cup sliced fennel bulb
- 1/2 cup sliced red peppers
- 1 cup sliced bok choy
- 1 Tbsp. coconut oil

Instructions

Marinade fennel in a Superfoods marinade. Stir fry drained fennel and celery in coconut oil for 4-5 more minutes. Add the rest of the marinade, bok choy and red peppers and stir fry for a minute. Serve with brown rice or quinoa.

Kale & Pumpkin Stir Fry

Serves 2

Ingredients - Allergies: SF, GF, DF, EF

- 1/2 pound Pumpkin
- 2 cups kale
- 1/2 cup onions
- 1 Tbsp. coconut oil

Instructions

Marinade pumpkin in a Superfoods marinade. Stir fry drained pumpkin in coconut oil for 4-5 more minutes. Add the rest of the marinade, onions and kale and stir fry for 2 minutes more. Serve with brown rice or quinoa.

Cauliflower & Green Onions Stir Fry
Serves 2

Ingredients - Allergies: SF, GF, DF, EF

- 1 pound cauliflower
- 1 cup green onions
- 1/2 tsp. chili flakes
- 1/2 cup onions
- 1 lime slice
- 1 Tbsp. coconut oil

Instructions

Marinade cauliflower in a Superfoods marinade and chili flakes. Stir fry drained cauliflower in coconut oil for 4-5 more minutes. Add the rest of the marinade, green onions and onions and stir fry for a minute. Decorate with lime slice and serve with brown rice or quinoa.

Kale & 2 Mushrooms Stir Fry
Serves 2

Ingredients - Allergies: SF, GF, DF, EF

- 1/2-pound shiitake and Portobello mushrooms
- 2 cups Kale
- 1/2 cup sliced onions
- 1 Tbsp. coconut oil

Instructions

Marinade shiitake in a Superfoods marinade. Stir fry drained shiitake and kale in coconut oil for few minutes, add all other vegetables and stir fry for 2 more minutes. Add the rest of the marinade and stir fry for a minute. Serve with brown rice or quinoa.

Kale, Carrot & Green Peas Stir Fry

Serves 2

Ingredients - Allergies: SF, GF, DF, EF

- 1/2 pound green peas
- 2 cups Kale
- 1/2 cup sliced Carrots
- 1/2 cup onion
- 1 Tbsp. coconut oil

Instructions

Marinade green peas in a Superfoods marinade. Stir fry drained green peas and kale in coconut oil for few minutes, add all vegetables and stir fry for 2 more minutes. Add the rest of the marinade and stir fry for a minute. Serve with brown rice or quinoa.

Water Chestnut, Broccoli, Carrots, Snow Peas & Shrimp Stir Fry

Serves 2

Ingredients - Allergies: SF, GF, DF, EF

- 1/2-pound shrimp
- 1/2 cup sliced water chestnut
- 1/2 cup sliced Onions
- 1/2 cup sliced carrots
- 1/2 cup sliced snow peas
- 1/2 cup sliced broccoli
- 1 Tbsp. oil

Instructions

Marinade shrimp in a Superfoods marinade. Stir fry drained shrimp in coconut oil for few minutes, add all vegetables and stir fry for 2 more minutes. Add the rest of the marinade and stir fry for a minute. Serve with brown rice or quinoa.

Yellow Squash, Broccoli, Snow Peas & Shiitake Stir Fry
Serves 2

Ingredients - Allergies: SF, GF, DF, EF

- 1/2-pound chicken
- 1/2 cup sliced yellow squash
- 1 cup sliced broccoli
- 1/2 cup sliced snow peas
- 1/2 cup sliced shiitake
- 1 Tbsp. oil

Instructions

Marinade chicken in a Superfoods marinade. Stir fry drained chicken in coconut oil for few minutes, add all vegetables and stir fry for 2 more minutes. Add the rest of the marinade and stir fry for a minute. Serve with brown rice or quinoa.

Zucchini, Green Beans, Leeks & Shrimp Stir Fry
Serves 2

Ingredients - Allergies: SF, GF, DF, EF
- 1/2 pound shrimp
- 1 cup sliced zucchini
- 1 cup sliced green beans
- 1/2 cup sliced leeks
- 1 Tbsp. oil

Instructions
Marinade shrimp in a Superfoods marinade. Stir fry drained shrimp in coconut oil for few minutes, add all vegetables and stir fry for 2 more minutes. Add the rest of the marinade and stir fry for a minute. Serve with brown rice or quinoa.

Green Beans, Sesame, Broccoli, Red Peppers & Portobello Stir Fry

Serves 2

Ingredients - Allergies: SF, GF, DF, EF

- 2 cups sliced green beans
- 1 cup broccoli
- 1/4 cup sesame seeds
- 1/2 cup sliced carrots and red peppers
- 1 Tsp. oil

Instructions

Marinade green beans in a Superfoods marinade. Stir fry drained green beans in coconut oil for few minutes, add all vegetables and stir fry for 2 more minutes. Add the rest of the marinade and stir fry for a minute. Serve with brown rice or quinoa.

Shiitake, Bamboo Shoots & Eggplant Stir Fry
Serves 2

Ingredients - Allergies: SF, GF, DF, EF

- 1/2 pound eggplant
- 1 cup sliced bamboo shoots
- 1 cup sliced shiitake
- 1/2 cup sliced onions
- 1 Tbsp. coconut oil
- 2 Tsp. sesame seeds and minced green onions each

Instructions

Marinade eggplant in a Superfoods marinade. Stir fry drained eggplant in coconut oil for few minutes, add onions, bamboo shoots and shiitake and stir fry for 2 more minutes. Add the rest of the marinade and stir fry for a minute. Decorate with green onions and sesame seeds. Serve with brown rice or quinoa.

Superfoods Reference Book

Unfortunately, I had to take out the whole Superfoods Reference Book out of all of my books because parts of that book are featured on my blog. I joined Kindle Direct Publishing Select program which allows me to have all my books free for 5 days every 3 months. Unfortunately, KDP Select program also means that all my books have to have unique content that is not available in any other online store or on the Internet (including my blog). I didn't want to remove parts of Superfoods Reference book that is already on my blog because I want that all people have free access to that information. I also wanted to be part of KDP Select program because that is an option to give my book for free to anyone. So, some sections of my Superfoods Reference Book can be found on my blog, under Superfoods menu on my blog. Complete Reference book is available for subscribers to my Superfoods Today Newsletter. Subscribers to my Newsletter will also get information whenever any of my books becomes free on Amazon. I will not offer any product pitches or anything similar to my subscribers, only Superfoods related information, recipes and weight loss and fitness tips. So, subscribe to my newsletter, download Superfoods Today Desserts free eBook which has complete Superfood Reference book included and have the opportunity to get all of my future books for free.

Your Free Gift

As a way of saying thanks for your purchase, I'm offering you my FREE eBook that is exclusive to my book and blog readers.

Superfoods Cookbook Book Two has over 70 Superfoods recipes and complements Superfoods Cookbook Book One and it contains Superfoods Salads, Superfoods Smoothies and Superfoods Deserts with ultra-healthy non-refined ingredients. All ingredients are 100% Superfoods.

It also contains Superfoods Reference book which is organized by Superfoods (more than 60 of them, with the list of their benefits), Superfoods spices, all vitamins, minerals and antioxidants. Superfoods Reference Book lists Superfoods that can help with 12 diseases and 9 types of cancer.

Other Books from this Author

Superfoods Today Diet is a Kindle Superfoods Diet book that gives you 4 week Superfoods Diet meal plan as well as 2 weeks maintenance meal plan and recipes for weight loss success. It is an extension of Detox book and it's written for people who want to switch to Superfoods lifestyle.

Superfoods Today Body Care is a Kindle book with over 50 Natural Recipes for beautiful skin and hair. It has body scrubs, facial masks and hair care recipes made with the best Superfoods like avocado honey, coconut, olive oil, oatmeal, yogurt, banana and Superfoods herbs like lavender, rosemary, mint, sage, hibiscus, rose.

Superfoods Today Cookbook is a Kindle book that contains over 160 Superfoods recipes created with 100% Superfoods ingredients. Most of the meals can be prepared in under 30 minutes and some are really quick ones that can be done in 10 minutes only. Each recipe combines Superfoods ingredients that deliver astonishing amounts of antioxidants, essential fatty acids (like omega-3), minerals, vitamins, and more.

Superfoods Today Smoothies is a Kindle Superfoods Smoothies book with over 70+ 100% Superfoods smoothies. Featured are Red, Purple, Green and Yellow Smoothies

Low Carb Recipes for Diabetics is a Kindle Superfoods book with Low Carb Recipes for Diabetics.

Diabetes Recipes is a Kindle Superfoods book with Superfoods Diabetes Recipes suitable for Diabetes Type-2.

Diabetic Cookbook for One is a Kindle Superfoods underline book with Diabetes Recipes for One suitable for Diabetes Type-2

Diabetic Meal Plans is a Kindle book with Superfoods Diabetes Meal Plans suitable for Diabetes Type-2

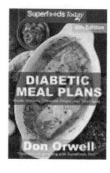

One Pot Cookbook is a Kindle Superfoods book with Superfoods One Pot Recipes.

Low Carb Dump Meals is a Kindle book with Low Carb Dump Meals Superfoods Recipes.

Superfoods Today Salads is a Kindle book that contains over 60 Superfoods Salads recipes created with 100% Superfoods ingredients. Most of the salads can be prepared in 10 minutes and most are measured for two. Each recipe combines Superfoods ingredients that deliver astonishing amounts of antioxidants, essential fatty acids (like omega-3), minerals, vitamins, and more.

Superfoods Today Kettlebells is a Kindle Kettlebells beginner's book aimed at 30+ office workers who want to improve their health and build stronger body without fat.

Superfoods Today Red Smoothies is a Kindle Superfoods Smoothies book with more than 40 Red Smoothies.

Superfoods Today 14 Days Detox is a Kindle Superfoods Detox book that gives you 2 week Superfoods Detox meal plan and recipes for Detox success.

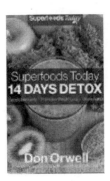

Superfoods Today Yellow Smoothies is a Kindle Superfoods Smoothies book with more than 40 Yellow Smoothies.

Superfoods Today Green Smoothies is a Kindle Superfoods Smoothies book with more than 35 Green Smoothies.

Superfoods Today Purple Smoothies is a Kindle Superfoods Smoothies book with more than 40 Purple Smoothies.

Superfoods Cooking For Two is a Kindle book that contains over 150 Superfoods recipes for two created with 100% Superfoods ingredients.

Nighttime Eater is a Kindle book that deals with Nighttime Eating Syndrome (NES). Don Orwell is a life-long Nighttime Eater that has lost his weight with Superfoods and engineered a solution around Nighttime Eating problem. Don still eats at night☺. Don't fight your nature, you can continue to eat at night, be binge free and maintain low weight.

Superfoods Today Smart Carbs 20 Days Detox is a Kindle Superfoods book that will teach you how to detox your body and start losing weight with Smart Carbs. The book has over 470+ pages with over 160+ 100% Superfoods recipes.

Superfoods Today Vegetarian Salads is a Kindle book that contains over 40 Superfoods Vegetarian Salads recipes created with 100% Superfoods ingredients. Most of the salads can be prepared in 10 minutes and most are measured for two.

Superfoods Today Vegan Salads is a Kindle book that contains over 30 Superfoods Vegan Salads recipes created with 100% Superfoods ingredients. Most of the salads can be prepared in 10 minutes and most are measured for two.

Superfoods Today Soups & Stews is a Kindle book that contains over 70 Superfoods Soups and Stews recipes created with 100% Superfoods ingredients.

Superfoods Desserts is a Kindle Superfoods Desserts book with more than 60 Superfoods Recipes.

Smoothies for Diabetics is a Kindle book that contains over 70 Superfoods Smoothies adjusted for diabetics.

50 Shades of Superfoods for Two is a Kindle book that contains over 150 Superfoods recipes for two created with 100% Superfoods ingredients.

50 Shades of Smoothies is a Kindle book that contains over 70 Superfoods Smoothies.

50 Shades of Superfoods Salads is a Kindle book that contains over 60 Superfoods Salads recipes created with 100% Superfoods ingredients. Most of the salads can be prepared in 10 minutes and most are measured for two. Each recipe combines Superfoods ingredients that deliver astonishing amounts of antioxidants, essential fatty acids (like omega-3), minerals, vitamins, and more.

Superfoods Vegan Desserts is a Kindle Vegan Dessert book with 100% Vegan Superfoods Recipes.

Desserts for Two is a Kindle Superfoods Desserts book with more than 40 Superfoods Desserts Recipes for two.

Superfoods Paleo Cookbook is a Kindle Paleo book with more than 150 100% Superfoods Paleo Recipes.

Superfoods Breakfasts is a Kindle Superfoods book with more than 40 100% Superfoods Breakfasts Recipes.

Superfoods Dump Dinners is a Kindle Superfoods book with Superfoods Dump Dinners Recipes.

Healthy Desserts is a Kindle Desserts book with more than 50 100% Superfoods Healthy Desserts Recipes.

Superfoods Salads in a Jar is a Kindle Salads in a Jar book with more than 35 100% Superfoods Salads Recipes.

Smoothies for Kids is a Kindle Smoothies book with more than 80 100% Superfoods Smoothies for Kids Recipes.

Vegan Cookbook for Beginners is a Kindle Vegan book with more than 75 100% Superfoods Vegan Recipes.

Vegetarian Cooking for Beginners is a Kindle Vegetarian book with more than 150 100% Superfoods Paleo Recipes.

Foods for Diabetics is a Kindle book with more than 170 100% Superfoods Diabetics Recipes.

Healthy Kids Cookbook is a Kindle book with Superfoods Kids friendly Recipes.

Superfoods Beans Recipes is a Kindle book with Superfoods Beans Recipes.

Diabetic Slow Cooker Recipes is a Kindle book with Superfoods Slow Cooker Diabetic Recipes.

Ketogenic Crockpot Recipes is a Kindle book with Superfoods Ketogenic Crockpot Recipes.

Stir Fry Cooking is a Kindle book with Stir Fry Superfoods Recipes.

Sirt Food Diet Cookbook is a Kindle book with Superfoods Sirt Food Recipes.

Made in the USA
Columbia, SC
30 June 2020